Her Voice

Hänen äänensä : a hybrid memoir

Faith Adiele

TRP: The University Press of SHSU

Huntsville, Texas

★trp

Library of Congress Control Number: 2024935247

Her Voice: Hänen Äänensä : a hybrid memoir
ISBN: 9781680033595 (paperback)
Cover & book design: PJ Carlisle
Front cover photo: MikeVon@unsplash.com & thevoncomplex.com
Title font: Afronaut by Mateusz Machalski, Poland
Printed and bound in the United States of America
FIRST EDITION
Printed and bound in the United States of America

the university press of shsu
huntsville, texas 77341
texasreviewpress.org

For Mummi, Mom, and Liisa, our first Americans

Contents

Hänen Äänensä
// Her Voice

Forty years after her death, my mummi//grandmother strolls into my dream. She emerges from a cloud of fog or smoke like a Film Noir heroine, her soft beak of a nose forming in mid-air above Cupid's bow lips. Breathless, I watch her profile approach in black and white.

I'm surprised. Not so much by her arrival—in our culture, our ancestors follow us and protect us—but by my ability to remember a dream.

Wow, my dreamself remarks. *You're actually remembering something; this is huge!*

Mummi Lempi turns to me and starts to set the table, with dishes or art supplies . . . it isn't yet clear. Her movements are as familiar as our very own Ingrid Bergman in *Gaslight*, in *Spellbound*, in *Notorious*, in *Casablanca*, always soft and cool. She's been gone too long, my doppelgänger, the one who made me an artist. The one who holds my left hand, the writing one, in her soft right one, her other hand still holding onto Finland. The one who bends over my bed at night, even if I can't see and don't remember, whispering. She whispers verses from the *Kalevala*, our national epic. She whispers the names of relatives lost in the project of im/migration. She whispers my work, all the things that I as our first Black-and-white-make-brown American must remember.

"Muistaa//Remember," I whisper to her. To myself.

Her last major visitation was almost thirty years ago, when I was deep in meditation in the Thai forest after a breakdown. No sooner had her face formed before my eyes, than it dissolved back into the dark, even as I called out, frantically pleading with her to return. I exited meditation, cheeks hot with tears, but the head nun smiled gently and told me not to worry. Mummi Lempi had come to tell me that she was okay. And I would be too.

This time, thank goodness, she's not so rushed. As she lingers, I suddenly realize that I've spent nearly three times as much of my life without her as I have with her. How can that be? She was so essential to the first twelve years of my life, especially once we moved to their farm.

Mummi, what would you like me to do? my dreamself asks, and she looks up from her tasks, smooth-faced, gentle as always.

She was the baby of her family, named for the Finnish god of Love. Smiling, she opens her mouth and starts to speak.

I squint and lean forward. I hear the muted, velvety darkness of dreamworld. Then a low hum.

Eventually the faint sounds of northern California waking up call me back: Dogs on leashes sniffing circles past each other. Children flatfooting towards school buses like mini-missiles. Aromatic taco trucks jingling into formation. The soft rasps of the man next to me.

And suddenly I'm upright in bed. Tangled in damp sheets. Gulping oxygen like someone who's just surfaced. My legs linger in the dreamworld, paralyzed with sleep. I claw at my nightdress. Squish a palm against my chest, desperate to feel, then quiet, the heartbird fluttering inside. Now I'm sobbing. Spumes of tears and snot soaking the bed. Alarming my partner, who's now awake.

"What is it?" he pleads. "What happened?"

I shake my head, not ready to voice it, though I know what the dream means. I can no longer hear my mummi. I've forgotten her voice.

Nordic Vowels

> The Finns inhale as they speak, a lovely sotto voce confirmation that two minds are in solemn agreement. Whispers and inhalations as twilight covers the city. I talk to the empty seat beside me and speak Finnish to an imaginary friend. . . . I exhale and speak in a flurry to my little doppelgänger.
>
> —*Stephen Kuusisto, "Night Song"*

As soon as my partner has departed for work, I call my mother. The minute I hear her voice on the phone, I'm bawling like a baby. Eventually, desperate, she threatens to call an ambulance. I feel like I can't breathe. Patting my chest with my right hand, as if soothing a baby, I steady the phone wobbling in my left hand and between gasps choke out the news that I can't remember Mummi Lempi's voice.

"Oh—?" She sounds cautious.

I must sound nuts. Who calls out of the blue, hysterical about a forty-year-old death? A Pisces, that's who! I describe the dream, and after a lifetime of dealing with Pisces, she adapts quickly.

"I'm sorry, sweetie," she says with a sad sigh. "Yes, most days I can't believe how long she's been gone. She was everything."

Now I feel like crying for my mom.

She sighs again, then giggles. "You know, when I was growing up, people always confused me for her on the phone."

That's strange. People confuse me for *my* mom on the phone. How can that be?

"I dunno," Mom says. "People *also* said she had a thick Finnish accent. I didn't hear that. I guess I was so used to it."

I guess I was too. I certainly don't remember a Finnish accent, even when I could still hear her voice.

"But at college," Mom continues, "these Norwegian students

marched right up to me and asked where I was from. I told them *here,* just three hours away, but they kept grilling me until I said my mother was Finnish and your morfar//grandfather was Swedish, but I didn't speak either language. They said, 'Aha! No matter! With *those* vowels, you clearly learned English from Scandinavians!'" She gives a delighted trickling laugh.

"Nordics," I correct, automatically advocating for Finns, who are always getting lumped in with Scandinavians. This makes even less sense. I'm half Nigerian, raised in America. How can I sound like my mom who sounded like Mummi Lempi who sounded Finnish?

I hang up and wrap myself in the past. I slip my finger into my mummi's diamond engagement ring with the band worn filigree-thin. I slide on her vintage Pendleton wool car coat with the red satiny lining that I'm terrified I'll misplace every time I wear it outside. I spend the rest of the day in bed, leafing through her hand-tinted photo albums, picturing what happened before and after each shot. Half the pages are blank, already looted by me. I am a hoarder of family artifacts, of what is lost in the act of im/migration and re/making. I have always relied on my senses to lead the way. The taste of words in my mouth, the way they accumulate on the page, building portals to the past. The lost emotions preserved in old bottles, just waiting for me to uncork and inhale. The ghostly indentations and traces of warmth left behind in used clothes.

But how do you go about recapturing the sound of a voice that no longer exists?

By evening, I'm pretty sure I should make a short film. Perhaps the images and movement can help recover her voice. Or at least help me process the act of forgetting her voice. I'm not sure. Do I know how to make a film?

Filmmaking for Listmakers

You come from a long line of champion listmakers. When your mom was trying to figure out how (as a single college student who'd just been disowned for getting pregnant) to keep you, she made a list. When your mummi realized she was dying, she made a list. Get your pad and pen; you can do this.

When learning to make a film, you can begin by taking stock of your inheritance. It isn't much, thanks to Morfar's Witch of a Second Wife, who tossed everything.

Your immigrant inheritance primarily consists of:

- ☑ Cotton pillowcases hand-embroidered and cross-stitched with flowers.
- ☑ A mismatched collection of pie tins and weights.
- ☑ A set of silver brushed-aluminum kitchen canisters with copper-colored lids.
- ☑ The good Arabia, pale blue dishes hand-painted in Finland with a green thistle design.
- ☑ Several embossed leather-bound journals of different sizes you managed to steal back from Uncle Michael-Väinö. They were yours anyway. As the only son, he inherited Morfar Gib's photos, while as the only daughter, your mother inherited Mummi Lempi's journals, but then he borrowed them and stopped talking to the two of you, so you had to make nice long enough to lure him to a family reunion where you asked to "borrow" the journals. Life in the New World without Mummi Lempi is downright exhausting.
- ☑ What you're already wearing.

Inheritance
Possessed

MY INHERITANCE
FROM MUMMI LEMPI:

My horoscope (Pisces, have mercy!)

Quiet art

The Kalevala

Sisu (the Finnish art of suffering stoicly)

Melancholy (we don't have to like it)

Bakeware. Hand-tinted photo albums. Handpainted Arabia dishes. Plaid car coat.

Natal homing

MY INHERITANCE
FROM MORFAR GIB:

My political outrage

Loud storytelling

Norse mythology. Vikings

Hot temper (when Sisu doesn't work)

Charm (when you lose family, make friends)

Cribbage board carved from Alaskan walrus tusks. WWII photojournalism.

Firm belief that Bag Balm will fix everything.

Lempi ~~Betty~~ & Gib   52

Her journals (which I had to trick my uncle into bringing to a family reunion and which I tossed into the car before speeding away, because nobody gonna take my inheritance)

A single DVD with footage from degraded home movies, a gift to Mom from the same uncle during one of his making amends performances. Not to be shared with me, the Black one who thinks she's so smart (nice try!).

I'm possessed. With good reason. I'm the only one of me.

There are younger siblings in Nigeria, fully African, raised by the father who left me behind, and Nordic cousins throughout America, Finland, and Sweden, but I'm the only one of me. As an only child with a single parent, I've always been terrified of being left behind. Whenever my friends threatened to leave home in search of their Real Parents Who Would Let Them Eat Candy for Dinner & Wouldn't Make Them Do Chores, I was dumbstruck. It never occurred to me to try to make it to the next town with a sandwich and a change of underpants; I was too busy worrying that my remaining parent might run away from home.

I'm damned if Mummi Lempi, the one who understood me, is going to leave me.

Filmmaking for Narcissists

☑ When learning to make a film, it's important to leave the doors and windows open. That way, the ancestors who follow you and protect your clan can send gifts your way.

☑ Receive a padded manila envelope from your mom. Inside the generic plastic drugstore case is a DVD.

☑ Call your Mom, who says it's from her brother, who turned up at her door out of the blue (after all these years!) and handed her a DVD. She chuckles. "He must've been feeling nostalgic. I wouldn't have even recognized him, except he had a white beard and looked like Dad!"

☑ Pause to consider this message and gift. Granted, it's a lot to process. Uncle Michael-Väinö looks like Morfar Gib? Morfar Gib had a video camera? Video footage of your family exists? You've never seen your family in action.

☑ Hand shaking, slide the DVD into your laptop and lean forward.

☑ Watch a montage of short domestic scenes, then press play again.

☑ Remind yourself to breathe. You've hit the jackpot. Nearly all the footage is Mummi Lempi.

☑ Log the scenes: There she is, as busy as you remember her. Mummi Lempi carrying armfuls of vegetables through the garden. Mummi Lempi setting up folding chairs for a picnic. Mummi Lempi pouring cups of kaffee for fika. Mummi Lempi even mowing the lawn in an A-line housedress (certainly staged)?

☑ Note a new character entering the frame: The teenager who will eventually become your mother makes a brief appearance in ponytail and pedal pushers, laughing as she dangles a line heavy with fresh-caught salmon above the cluster of attentive farm cats at her feet.

☑ Watch to the end. Note a single sequence with Mummi Lempi, her sister Täti Rauha, and you. You! Not only is it the only video you've ever seen of you, all of you, but it means that the footage spanned over a decade. How did you forget that Morfar was filming for years?

☑ Log this sole video footage of you as a child: You're wearing a short Afro and a green swimsuit with white polka dots, short pleated skirt, and ruffles across your chest. In one shot, you're staring at the camera as you climb into an inflatable donut in a small pool. In another, you clamber onto a picnic table in the backyard, a hula hoop clasped in one hand. Mummi Lempi and Täti Rauha are clearly getting ready for a summer cookout or family birthday. Mummi is wearing a bright flowered house dress and has a filmy scarf draped over a head full of curlers. She is busy setting out folding lawn chairs, while Täti tugs at the tablecloth and starts to set the table.

☑ Study the screen intently: Unable to get Mummi's and Täti's attention, child-you mugs cheekily at the camera. At you.

Filmmaking for
Amateur Sleuths

When learning to make a film, it may take you a minute to realize who is missing from the home-movie footage. Hint: it's the men. You know the deal; make the list:

- ☑ One, your disappeared-to-Africa father, who was never there in the first place.
- ☑ Two, Uncle Michael-Väinö, who—what with the Drinking & the Drugging & the Staying Out All Night with Friends & the Sleeping Until Afternoon—might as well have not been there.
- ☑ Three, Morfar Gib, the invisible director and cameraman behind the scenes. The expert fisherman who caught and is going to smoke the skein of salmon in your mother's hands in an old fridge he outfitted with a chimney and smoke generator. It stands outside the bunkhouse, just waiting for you to tug it open on your way to and from the farmhouse, stick your nose inside, and inhale the fatty, salty, smoky perfume of salmon until your eyes water with joy.

PRO TIP: All you need is an old refrigerator, some charcoal, wood chips, drill, old pipe, metal bucket, source of power, and you too can build your cold smoker and bring your morfar back to life.

When learning to make a film, it may take you a minute to realize what is missing from the footage. Hint: it's sound.

You press hard on the volume icon, the pressure dull against the pad of your index finger, and are rewarded with the low whirr of gears and white noise.

《◈〉- - 《◈〉- - 《◈〉- - 《◈〉- - 《◈〉- - 《◈〉

《◈〉- - 《◈〉- - 《◈〉- - 《◈〉- - 《◈〉- - 《◈〉

《◈〉- - 《◈〉- - 《◈〉- - 《◈〉- - 《◈〉- - 《◈〉

Your heart starts to thump, and you eject the DVD with fingers that tremble, clean it with a microfiber, and start again.

《◈〉- - 《◈〉- - 《◈〉- - 《◈〉- - 《◈〉- - 《◈〉

《◈〉- - 《◈〉- - 《◈〉- - 《◈〉- - 《◈〉- - 《◈〉

《◈〉- - 《◈〉- - 《◈〉- - 《◈〉- - 《◈〉- - 《◈〉

Nothing.
　　　These are silent home movies.
　　　　　Silent.
　　　　　　　Utterly soundless.

Like the movies Mummi Lempi grew up on. Like your dream, your memory. It's a haunting, not source material.

The Underworld

I believe maybe life everlasting is achieved by love. Since
we aren't forgotten by the people who knew and loved us.
How wonderful to be able to think about the experiences
we had with people even after they are gone. Maybe we
can't see them again but they will always live in our memory.

—*Mummi Lempi's Diary, 1974*

Mummi Lempi strides out of the Underworld and crosses center
screen at dusk. There she is, in a deep blue shirtwaist dress, head-
ing towards the T-bar of the laundry line in our familiar backyard.
She exits screen left, barely discernible through my tears. Or is
the DVD glitching? Or the original film from which the DVD
was copied?

I press pause. White holes pockmark the screen like lace. It's
not the DVD. The film was degrading, just like my memory. Uncle
Michael-Väinö, despite his flaws, caught it just in time.

I hit play again, and somewhere in the Pacific Northwest, a
young Mummi Lempi in a short-sleeve white blouse and dark skirt
approaches a stone lookout point. She cranes her neck delicately,
revealing a pointed chin, and leans toward the view. As she gazes
down, the camera follows her sightline, panning along an arched
bridge and then down into a deep, rocky gorge.

I'm not sure the landscape is lush enough to be the famous
Deception Pass Bridge, a graceful set of steel arches linking the
Whidbey and Fidalgo Islands. Deception is over the Cascade
Mountains, but only four hours northwest and in the direction of
the Swedish side of the family.

The other possibility is the Twin Falls-Jerome Bridge (since
renamed the I. B. Perrine Bridge), which rises a stunning 486 feet

above the twisting Snake River Canyon. But it's southeast, seven hours away in why-would-anyone-want-to-go-there southern Idaho.

For some odd reason, the film at the bottom of the screen is slightly colorized. It's as if Mummi had gotten to it with her

TWIN FALLS-JEROME BRIDGE, 1500 FT. LONG, 475 FT. HIGH, IDAHO—16

Property of University of Washington Libraries, Special Collections Division

delicate photo brushes, revealing a cobalt-blue river, edged with greenery. By the time the camera swings back, Mummi Lempi has already turned away and is striding toward the open door of a pale, big-finned car.

Away from Morfar Gib. Away from the camera. Away from me.

Filmmaking for Researchers

When learning to make a film, acknowledge that there will be bumps in the road. Set aside the home movies for now. You still need a soundtrack, and despite the fact that Mummi Lempi didn't speak English until she went to primary school and didn't graduate high school and never learned to write Finnish, her English-language diaries may still be your best bet for resurrecting her voice. What clues lie within the worn, gilt-edged, stolen-back journals?

☑ Read the diaries if you dare. Hunt for her voice in the black-and-blue loops and slanted lines on the page. Can you hear her, almost? She's getting stronger in memory but weaker on the page. The decline starts May, 1972. Why May 1972? Strap on a spotlight and follow her down a research rabbit hole.

☑ May 1972 begins with death. As a construction foreman, your morfar is obsessed with news about the fire at the Sunshine Mine, just four hours away in Idaho. After hauling out eighty men, the hoist operator dies on the spot of gas inhalation, and the remaining ninety-one silver miners perish.

☑ May 1972 ends with a crime, no, two—one medical, one political. Both US President Nixon and Soviet leader Brezhnev want to détente, to de-escalate, of which you approve. Dick flies to Moscow to sign SALT I, a treaty limiting development of nuclear missiles. It's historic! Two days later, spies working to re-elect Nixon burglarize Democratic national headquarters back in Washington, DC. The diaries remind you that's all Mom and Morfar could talk about: WATERGATE. They're shocked shocked shocked but not surprised.

☑ Find news footage of the Watergate hearings. With audio. Watch a 1982 program that looks back at Watergate. One of the television news anchors looks arrestingly like Mummi Lempi, in clip-on pearls and a bob of sponge-roller waves that Grace Kelly made glamorous and Margaret Thatcher turned into a helmet. You can't believe your luck! But when you click on the video, the voice is Generic Midwestern Newscaster Monotone. "The most intense political crisis of our time began just ten years ago," she intones, "with the break-in at the Watergate hotel." Next!

☑ John Dean, Nixon's White House Counsel who first helped cover up Watergate and later turned state's witness, delivers the goods. His Senate testimony starts, "I began by telling the president that there was a cancer growing on the presidency. . . ."

Cancer! The diaries confirm what you remember: Cancer murdered Mummi. Cancer is the real villain in this story.

Filmmaking for Boom Operators

> Sometimes one thinks things are forgotten but a sight, smell or sound will bring them back. I remember walking one winter night to the movie theater at the other end of town. The snow on both sides of the sidewalk was piled six or seven feet high. Our feet crunched in the snow and it seemed like we were in a tunnel of white. It brings back my childhood when I walk in the snow and smell the cold wet.
>
> —*Mummi Lempi's Diaries, 1973*

☑ Heed the clue in her diaries: assemble a domestic soundtrack. What is the correct ambient noise to call childhood out of its tunnel of white?

☑ Set up the looks-like-Gumby desktop tripod you received as a promotional giveaway and use your iPhone to shoot footage of sugar sifting into Mummi Lempi's brushed aluminum canisters. It sounds like feet crunching over snow. Metal pie weights falling into her tin pie pans sound like rain on the roof of the barn and bunkhouse. Inhale sharply. This is perhaps your most successful attempt at filmmaking. You can almost hear her crunching footsteps approach.

☑ Go online to buy audio clips of Finnish and Swedish folk music, the nyckelharpa sounding like a fiddle and a harp had a baby, the accordion giving your Mom PTSD because Morfar came home with a mini-accordion when she was a child and forced her to take lessons.

☑ Buy audio clips of sound effects: the faraway buzz of lawnmowers, the hiss of water hitting hot coals in the sauna. Feel your Nordic muscles instinctively loosen and relax.

☑ Pray that this is the correct alchemy. Pray that it will be enough to summon Mummi Lempi from the Underworld.

Pisces Fish Girls

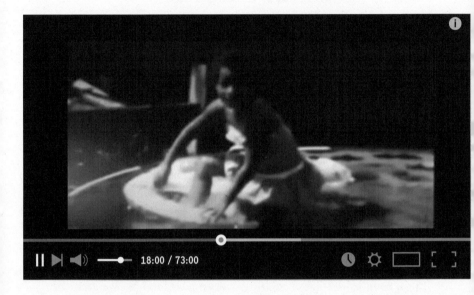

⏸ ⏭ 🔊 ——●—	18:00 / 73:00	🕐 ☼ ▭ ⸢ ⸥

Mummi Lempi and I are Pisces, born exactly five days and fifty years apart. A matched set of dreamy, artistic types, according to the daily horoscope she checks over her second cup of Postum and reads aloud while I get started on art. Weepy, too-sensitive fish-girls, as we will learn outside the house.

Inside the house, we sit together at the sunny kitchen table, missing countries and ancestors we've never seen, sculpting, baking, molding, painting: watercolor on rocks, semi-transparent oil on photos, food-colored egg wash on Joulu cookies.

She glances up from the *Yakima Herald*, finally ready to speak. Do I know how her memory-dreamvoice sounds?

"Oh, today's horoscope is verrry good," she says.

She sounds like Mummi, but what is that? It's more a feeling than an accent, as if I'm feeling her words vibrate in my brain and heart rather than through my ears. But I also know that each first syllable must've been emphasized.

"You could IL-lustrate a CHILD-ren's book, or your LET-ter to the ED-itor gets PUB-lished!"

We giggle. We'll take children's books; Mom and Morfar Gib are the ones sending weekly enraged letters to the *Herald*'s editor.

In my world there are two seasons that matter: Juhannus// Summer and Joulu//Christmas. In the summer, when there is no school, Morfar Gib sets up adult and kiddie pools in the abandoned pasture. Mummi Lempi and I gather wildflowers for Juhannus (which Morfar calls Midsommar, because Swedish makes sense, unlike Finnish, which makes no sense at all). Long evenings stretch into long games of tag and hide-and-seek with all the kids in the neighborhood racing through the cornfields and jumping off haystacks, joyful calls of "Olly olly oxen free" carrying all along Route 2.

But Joulu (which Morfar Gib calls Jul) is even better, with St. Lucia Day and four Sundays of adventti and nearly all December devoted to cookie baking. Twenty-four days of toasting trays of almonds and walnuts. Twenty-four days of defrosting Cool Whip containers of frozen berries and boiling them down into jewel-colored jams that spit and spatter the stove. Twenty-four days of creaming butter and almond extract into sugar crystals and sifting down clouds of flour. Twenty-four days of rolling out smooth sheets of dough with the ice-filled glass rolling pin and pressing tin cookie cutters of nissu, little Swedish pigs, and six-point stars.

Before baking, we paint the dough with tiny brushes, after which Mummi Lempi recites *Kalevala* to distract me during the baking. In our national epic, the powerful Matriarch of the North hides the sun and the moon and steals fire away from the people of the *Kalevala*, who will become the Finns. This is supposed to be bad from a Finnish nationalist standpoint, but since the future-Finns are patriarchal, we women are rooting for her.

There's a reason Mummi likes to sing the part about folk hero Väinämöinen who looks like a Viking and has to recover the fire from the belly of a pike, but I'll only learn that later. In the meantime, I like it because it's like the Old Lady Who Swallowed a Fly, but with fish.

Then finally, when the toasty aroma of butter and nuts and sugar is nearly unbearable, the kitchen timer DINGS! and Mummi Lempi flips open the double oven doors with a CLINK and a wave of heat. Sheet after sheet emerges, egg paint set in a deep, satiny glaze: Pigs spotted azure. Orange snowmen. Emerald, almond-scented stars. Success!

Grandmother
on Fire

As toddlers, both Mummi Lempi and I were nearly killed. Because it is written in the *Kalevala*. (Or because our respective mothers were alone and poor.) In either case, her near-death experience is my inheritance.

"Shall I tell you about The Hiding of the Sun and Moon ?" **Mummi Lempi asks, beginning the** *Kalevala:*

> Soon the fish that gulped the fire
> Felt a fiery ache within it
> The devourer full of anguish,
> Torment in the one who ate it.

I've always pictured moon-faced Mummi catching fire during Joulu or Juhannus with their festive Christmas and Midsommar pyres, but eventually I discovered that it was just a couple of neighborhood boys burning shit.

In my mind the entire Finnish immigrant community clustered on the shores of Lake Erie, where my imagined fire raged, tall as a house, flames leaping up the ends of twisted tree branches and shards of fishing boats, akvaviitti barrels and broken tanning scrapers. It sputtered, sucking the wind off the lake, and popped, sparks raining down like swarms of summer fireflies. Waves gasped in the distance, bottles clinked over low conversation, yams roasted sweetly.

Like one of the ravenous stray dogs that hung around outside the tanneries where the Finnish men worked, a flame darted forward to drag its tongue across Baby Lempi's belly. Startled, the toddler who will eventually become my mummi staggered back from the bonfire and with a whimper, burst into flame.

Screams pierced the velvety silence as the adults bolted across the sand towards her, and the memory disappears in a puff of smoke.

Perfume

As a toddler I am nearly killed. Because as a toddler Mummi Lempi was nearly killed. Because it is written in the *Kalevala*. Because it is my inheritance. Because Mummi Lempi and I are five days and fifty years apart.

I awake from dreamless afternoon sleep and track a rare beam of Seattle sun through the window. I totter towards the Scandia-design chest of drawers, blond wood that looks shellacked in honey. Perhaps the cloying scent of Coty cream and Avon perfume wafts down like wildflowers atop nearby Mount Rainier. Perhaps my mother has collected bottles of candy-colored nail polish and rhinestone brooches to remind her of the farm, two hundred miles away, across the mountains.

Several drawers jut out, exposing meager contents: The bottom drawer is open the furthest. The next drawer glows red with toddler tights and snap-crotch trousers. Each drawer opens a little less, together forming a smooth staircase.

I step into the bottom drawer, feeling itchy sweaters between my toes, and find my balance. My next step up settles onto trousers, the synthetic folds sinking beneath the pads of my feet, the metal snaps cold against my heels. In the drawer of balled-up socks and tights, I wobble a bit and grab the smooth round knobs on the drawer above.

Suddenly I feel a lurch. The bureau groans like a ship bound for America and sways. Then it jolts violently and flings me. I'm soaring through space, my stomach rushing up into my throat like when my babysitter isn't looking, and her daughter pushes me as high as the swings can go. I'm weightless, watching the heavy bureau flip. Then I'm not.

I hit the bedroom floor with a thud and a loud OOF (like

a cartoon bubble above me) followed by the crash of wood and shattering of glass. The back of my head, my shoulder blades, and my tailbone all throb. I gasp for breath, the back of my shirt wet, an acrid cloud of rose petals and acetone pinning me in place.

My college-student mother, a highlighter in each fist, shrieks and leaps up from the kitchen table. As her pens and heavy Poly Sci textbook slam on the linoleum and scatter, she speeds down the hall, reaching the bedroom doorway in seconds.

There I lie, crumpled on the floor beneath the bureau, surrounded by a sea of perfume and broken glass.

Screaming, she charges into the room, alone in this parenting thing. Her bare feet leave a perfumed trail of bloody footprints. *"Faith! Faith!"* she shouts.

Reaching me, she kneels atop the glass shards, praying to Eir the Healer, Frigga's handmaid, the Valkyrja who follows on the battlefield, deciding who will heal and who will die. "Eir!" she calls, "Have mercy!" She grabs my small shoulder and tugs. The smell is overpowering; her cut feet and knees sting with perfume.

I slip out as gooey and smelly as the moment of birth, but easier, no forceps this time. She snatches me up and runs shaking fingers over my face and through my curls, frantically searching for cuts. I'm streaked with blood, but it's hers, not mine. She palpates my arms and legs as if I were one of my carefully chosen, anatomically correct baby dolls with brown plastic skin, feeling for breaks and fractures.

She's still shouting my name, all the way to the Underworld, begging Eir and the Goddess Hel to let me go, and finally my eyes pop open. "Hi Mommy!" rings out. Impossibly. Brightly. Too damn cheerful, in fact.

And finally she sees the angled drawer that jammed the fall, holding the entire bureau over me like Yggdrasil, the sacred tree bearing up the nine worlds, itself. With a guttural cry of relief that starts from the womb, she clasps me to her breast. *"Thank you, Eir!"*

Grandma Moses
&
Mummi

Whenever Mom loses herself in a book, which is pretty much most of the time, I sneak out of our avocado-and-goldenrod-colored mobile home and scurry across the lush backyard to my grandparents' daffodil-yellow-on-the-outside, pastel-sorbet-on-the-inside farmhouse. I sprint up the concrete backstairs, slam the screen door and crouch in the hall, head swiveling left and right. I'm like Lady, our black-and-white sheepdog, sniffing out something in need of herding. I hear Mummi Lempi in the living room, watching her "Stories" on the big Zenith console TV, and dart right. There she is, sitting down for once, in the dim carpeted room, a wooden hoop in her hands and skeins of jeweled embroidery thread trailing down her legs.

She glances up, blue eyes sparkling beneath gray pin-curls, and grins, patting her thigh. I spring forward and wedge myself onto her soft calico lap, nose to housedress: Vanilla, cardamom, rye. She's been baking Finland again.

"Mummi, what're you doing?"

"Embroidering pillowcases," she explains in her singsong accent.

Is it singsong? am I really hearing her?

"Why do the houses and animals look so funny?"

"It is naïf." Her hands abandon her work and move gently through my curls, twisting curlicues around her thick farmwife fingers. "Grandma Moses. My favorite."

"Why?"

"She is example for old people."

"Why?"

"She vas farm wife. Then, in her seventies, she taught herself to paint."

I look up at her soft nose and former-beauty-queen lips. "She taught herself?"

"Yes!" Eyes bright, Mummi Lempi plants a kiss on my nose. "People say elderly cannot do things, but vhen she vas one hundred—"

"A hundred!"

"Yes! At one hundred, she illustrated 'Twas the Night Before JOU-lu,'"

"The Night Before Joulu! I love Christmas!"

She disentangles her hand from my curls, takes my fingers in her soft ones and places them on the scene she's embroidering.

"See?"

Together we trace horses and cows the same size as the barns that are supposed to house them. I can almost feel her hand on mine. It's the same way Morfar Gib, my Swedish grandfather, teaches me the hambo, placing my feet atop his cowboy boots then flying us in triple-time turns around the living room to the nyckelharpa and accordion music zithering its way out of the stereo console.

I nod and lean back into her warmth, memorizing: Cinnamon, Postum, soapy hair gel. Purple horses, green sky, art.

Grandmother as Camera

When Baby Lempi awakes, seas of panic slosh inside her fiery belly. She shrieks. It is her first pain. She doesn't know what's in store for a female immigrant body.

"Hush, hush," her mother sing-songs softly. "Mitä kuuluu//How are you?"

Her hand, the burned hand of a peasant-turned-washerwoman, a soon-to-be-single-mother-and-bootlegger, spreads silver nitrate, the newest burn remedy, over my future mummi's blistered belly.

Just like bonfire magic, which grants maidens the ability to dream of their future husbands, Baby Lempi sees her husband-to-be, a Swedish-American photojournalist smearing square plates with a silver paste like the one on her belly and holding them up to the light.

Baby Lempi blinks those blue-blue eyes rapidly and coughs, bringing the fire back to her belly, where it lives. She can feel the skin tightening, itching to reveal a new, shiny self beneath. Who is this girl, who will have to take a new name and learn to speak English at school? Will she be the same person, with these images in her belly, wrapped in scarlet-and-blue *Kalevala* clew, hardening? When will the scar tissue transform into cancerous silence?

All Us Hotheads

Mummi Lempi is the one holding all us hotheads together. I'm not yet as hot as I will eventually become (if Mom and Morfar Gib are any indication), but Mummi Lempi is definitely the one I adore, and each of *them* has always loved her more than the other.

Ditto for Uncle Michael-Väinö (*if* he were capable of noticing any of us, my mother says, Mummi Lempi would be the one). None of us is too fond of waspish, wound-tight-as-a-drum Täti Rauha (or whichever of her husbands is currently feuding with Morfar Gib), but Täti and Mummi Lempi are inseparable. "You have to understand," my mother says, "Täti was the only one who spoke and wrote English. Their mother was working all the time. Täti was left in charge of Mummi and their brother." Now she doesn't know how to stop being bossy. I understand. But I love Mummi Lempi.

A BRIEF SIDEBAR ABOUT SALMON

Some American science: After spending years swimming in the ocean, salmon follow their noses and return to the freshwater streams they were born in to spawn and eventually die.

They swim upstream against strong currents for hundreds of miles to make the perfect home-coming, even if it means arriving in shoddy condition.

Some Norse mythology: After causing the death of Baldr, god of light and peace, Tricster Loki shapeshifted into a salmon to escape the gods and hid beneath the waterfall.

When he jumped high into the air, like the salmon returning home to breed, Thor grabbed him and held firm, the pressure from the fist of the god of thunder and war forming the salmon's thin tail.

—*Corey Binns, "Top 10 Most Incredible Animal Journeys,"* Live Science, *May 25, 2007.*

My Colored Family

Mummi Lempi colors our family. I lean over the yellow Formica to watch.

(Sadly, today, my camera takes color photographs, all the work and fun already done. The only Black-and-white-make-brown one in the family, I still prefer this color that comes not from the world but from the artist.)

It's a family affair:

Morfar Gib takes the photos and develops them himself in a red room out in the bunkhouse that smells of chemicals; Mummi Lempi colors them and puts them in the family album; Mom takes them out, curating one definitive album with precise, hand-lettered captions and dates.

I want in.

Tiny paint brushes in her soft, square hands, like the ones we use for cookies, Mummi Lempi dabs tints onto Morfar Gib's scenes. The cardstock surfaces transform, the colors sugary, near edible: pastels like puddings made of whipped marja berry; the golden glaze of lussekatter//saffron buns.

"Your turn." She hands me workbooks with beige, porous pages that sop up watercolors.

I follow her lead, but her world out-enchants mine: My toddler mother in a Little Bo Peep-blue bonnet and marjapuuro-pink sweater leans against Mummi Lempi in a lemon-meringue dress. Nearby a child's chair glows red in a jade forest of grass. Occasionally the paint bleeds outside the lines: an intense blur hovers, each of us colored by her own personal aura.

Once my mother finishes assembling her family album, I snatch the photos that didn't make the cut: Mummi Lempi holding up her skirt to reveal shocking pink pantaloons; the luminous portrait of her as Snow Princess in 1935. Uncle Michael-Väinö in one of the cowboy outfits he lived in for most of his childhood. Mom at various ages, invariably holding an armful of squirming kittens. Outside the North Pole's Arctic Cafe, Morfar shivers in snow as high as his neck, hat tilted rakishly over his prematurely receding hairline.

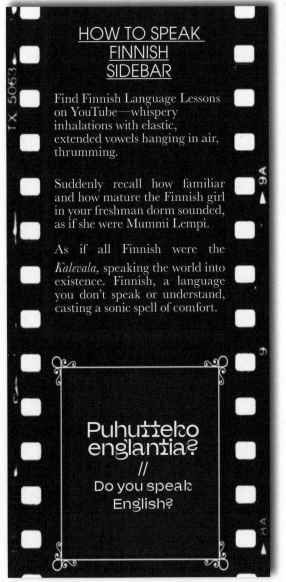

HOW TO SPEAK FINNISH SIDEBAR

Find Finnish Language Lessons on YouTube—whispery inhalations with elastic, extended vowels hanging in air, thrumming.

Suddenly recall how familiar and how mature the Finnish girl in your freshman dorm sounded, as if she were Mummi Lempi.

As if all Finnish were the *Kalevala,* speaking the world into existence. Finnish, a language you don't speak or understand, casting a sonic spell of comfort.

Puhutteko englantia?
//
Do you speak English?

Grandmother in High School

In 1972, the year Nixon and Agnew trounce our candidates in the largest landslide in U.S. history (a victory later besmirched by Watergate, serves them *goddamn* right!), the year Congress (but never the Senate) passes the ERA, declaring dangerously that, *Equality of rights under the law shall not be denied or abridged by the United States or any state on account of sex,* Mummi Lempi goes back to high school.

Why?

Let's be honest, I'm too young to care, too young to realize that though we all debate, analyze, write and read voraciously—books from the library, newspapers, magazines, pamphlets—Mom is the only one who's gone to college. I'm especially too young to know that Mummi Lempi knows she's on borrowed time. It's not just Mummi being busy as usual.

In the afternoons.   After serving breakfast.
Packing lunches for all of us. And driving my mother to work.
After mid-morning caffeklatch with Täti Rauha
After scrubbing, vacuuming & dusting the entire house
        top to bottom.
After the household laundry & ironing
(including Morfar's handkerchiefs).
After running our errands in town, picking me up from school
& driving me to piano lessons.
After weeding the garden & starting dinner.
She does her homework.
In the evenings, instead of going with Morfar to visit

The Athertons
The Stanlees
The Masons
The Schuts
The Faulks
The Giffins.
Instead of going round & square dancing.
Instead of staying home to ride horses, host bridge club, play
       board games.
Instead of the late movie & dinner with Täti Rauha & Uncle
       Whosit.
  She heads off quietly to class.

And despite weekly trips to the library for stacks of books.
Weekly American Legion, Democratic Club & other civic
       meetings.
Despite election board.
A steady stream of kids for dinner & sleepovers.
Weekends of farm work or camping or hunting trips.
Despite baking a pie
      from scratch
           every day
               for two decades.
  At age sixty-one, Mummi Lempi earns her GED.

One year later she is dead.

How to Bake a Pie

- ☑ Using your Mummi's pastry cutter with the flaking red handle, cut cold, unsalted butter into sifted flour with smooth wrist movements like hers until it resembles Bisquick.
- ☑ Add Crisco and rub with a thumb, forefinger and middle finger that don't resemble hers.
- ☑ Sprinkle in ice water, stirring with a tarnished silver fork, one Tbsp at a time, until the dough pulls away from the sides of the bowl and forms a ball.

"Shall I tell you about The Capture of the Fire?" Mummi Lempi asks from the Underworld, while you wait for the dough to chill.

That old fish story.
The hero Väinämöinen
Splits the gray pike wide open
In the belly of the gray pike he finds
The silver lake-trout
In the belly of the silver lake-trout he finds
The sleek-skinned white-fish.
In the gutbend of the whitefish,
Are three coils, and when this one was unraveled,
From the blue clew fell a red one.
When the red clew was unraveled
In its middle was the fire-spark
Which had fallen from the heavens.

- ☑ Using your Mummi's brushed aluminum flour shaker with the black top, sift flour over the quartz countertop.
- ☑ Roll out disks of chilled dough, turning and flipping, with

your tapered French rolling pin, wishing you had her antique glass one instead.

☑ Once it's smooth and nearly translucent, place a circle of dough in one of Mummi's glass or tin pie pans, pressing gently into the sides, then fill with fresh fruit from your berry patch or the neighbor's orchards and cover with a second circle.

☑ Using your left pointer finger on one side of the ridge of dough, and the thumb and pointer finger of your right hand on the other side, press to make even indentations along the entire edge of the crust.

☑ Spin the glass pie pan smoothly, feeling your Mummi's speed and strength as you crimp.

☑ When finished, brush milk atop the top and sprinkle with coarse sugar. Vent with a small paring knife.

☑ Start the crying now.

☑ Everyone knows her cookies (fourteen Joulu varieties, ice box, bar, pan, roll, drop, gun), and breads (limppu, banana, pulla, zucchini, nissua), and pies (Yakima Valley apple, strawberry-rhubarb, Yakima Valley peach, Oregon huckleberry, lemon meringue, Oregon blueberry, chocolate cream, Washington marionberry, banana cream, Yakima Valley cherry)—can make a grown man weep.

What I Didn't Know

Mom and Morfar Gib are whispering in the living room, heads bent together, the strong sun streaming through the picture window.

"She's been asleep all afternoon," Mom murmurs.

Up I leap, tossing down *Johnny Tremain*, which I'm reading for the third time. "I'll wake Mummi!" I shout.

I blast down the hall, past the laundry room, kitchen, and bathroom, around the laundry hamper at the end of the hall outside Uncle Michael-Väinö's room, and into the Pink Room (an all-purpose anteroom housing my piano and toys, Mummi Lempi's sewing machine and writing desk, and the storage closets).

I shove the pink-curtained French doors that stick and slip into the primary bedroom. There's something magical about this end of the house, particularly in the dim quiet of afternoon, when the sea foam and dusty rose walls sound like underwater silence, like a bubbling aquarium. Here, it smells like Joulu all year long, a combination of Old Spice, menthol rub, and pomanders I make by studding oranges with whole cloves and hanging them from satin ribbons in the large closets.

Mummi Lempi is asleep, little baby snores, so I rifle the closets, sniffing deeply for citrus and allspice. One closet, devoted entirely to Mummi Lempi's dance outfits, refuses to close. I poke a stiff pink petticoat inside, only to have an embroidered sleeve pop out. A triangular-shaped closet is packed with board games, jigsaw puzzles and paint-by-number kits, useless without Mummi Lempi to bring them to life.

I park myself on the plush mauve stool before her vanity, looking straight out of an old black-and-white musical, with its sleek blond wood and huge circular mirror. The glass surface sparkles with pots of Dippity-Do Gelée, the bright pink and blue gels smelling of Mummi Lempi fresh from the shower. After that, I move to the drawers spilling glittering costume jewelry and a rainbow of embroidery skeins.

Next I tiptoe to Morfar's dresser, littered with all sorts of strange and useless things I know by heart: Bottles of Old Spice aftershave, each with a single good swig left, broken Timex watches I carry off to the mobile home to dismantle and hoard in a box, their ticking silenced, square pink-and-green tins of Bag Balm. A thick ointment for cows and the maids who milk them, Bag Balm looks and smells like cake batter. Morfar Gib loves to tout its miraculous powers. "Let me tell you something——" he'd always say upon finding me in his bed, nose in the tin, about to lick one of the creamy whirls to see if it tastes like it smells——"I ran my thumb through the circular saw last week——" he'd spread his broad, scarred hands like the impresario he is and let his voice sink to a stage whisper——"It was hanging on by a *single* tendon."

"Eww!" I scrunch my eyes and try to imagine the wonderful, bloody scene.

"Well," he continues, tipping back his cap and winking a blue eye. "And this is the absolute truth. I scooped on some Bag Balm, bandaged it up, and the next day——*poof!*——not even a scar. *Completely* healed!" His powerful fingers wriggle, free of imaginary bandages. "Bag Balm."

"Stranger tings have happened," Mummi Lempi confirms, when I dash to the kitchen to check with her. "Particularly if your morfar is telling the story."

«⟡«

Mummi Lempi doesn't stir.

I jump onto the bed, feeling its give at my knees, and run my palms over the soft, rose-colored tufts. Chenille radiates out from her arm in swirls. I stare. The arm looks smaller than the one I remember only months ago digging iris bulbs before winter.

I touch it. It's dry, cooler than usual. The skin is so paper-thin, I can imagine peeling it right off the bone.

I shake the arm. It flops loosely, light. Mummi Lempi does not respond.

"*Mummi Lempi!*" I cry. My voice sounds like brittle shards ripping through the velvety room.

After a long moment, she opens one dull eye, and even I, transplanted-from-the-city farm girl that I am, have witnessed enough returned glassy-eyed salmon at the top of the stream, enough barn cats who've dragged themselves away from the others, to recognize the look.

I'm not ready.

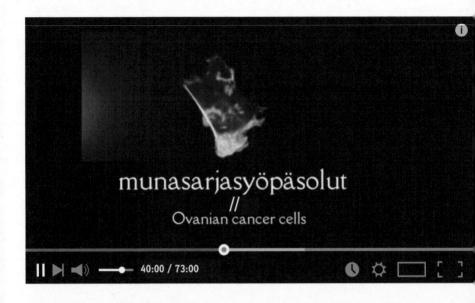

munasarjasyöpäsolut
//
Ovanian cancer cells

40:00 / 73:00

Minuun sattuu
//
I'm hurt

40:07 / 73:00

Watergate

I began by telling the president that there was a cancer growing on the presidency and that if the cancer was not removed that the President himself would be killed by it. I also told him that it was important that this cancer be removed immediately because it was growing more deadly every day.

—*John Dean, US Senate Hearings*
February 8, 1973

We gather in the living room, Morfar Gib in his recliner, the rest of us draped over the arms or sprawled at his feet. It's finally happening! Morfar and Mom are giddy, hands flying, cheeks pink, voices loud. Tricky Dick and his cronies are finally going to get their comeuppance! The truth will out. It's more exciting than Election Night.

Tires squeal in the driveway, followed by the metallic slam of a car door, the crunch of gravel and the tinny clatter of the backdoor. Uncle Michael-Väinö rushes in, cheeks flushed pink above his droopy blond mustache. "Has it started?"

He hands a Family Bucket from KFC to my mother and goes to grab two beers from the fridge. The rich oily smell of fried chicken fills the air. Mummi Lempi, wan and quiet in the corner, hasn't been cooking. Mom hands around styrofoam containers of mashed potatoes and coleslaw, tiny corn on the cob and a drumstick for me. Uncle Michael-Väinö returns to the living room and hands Morfar Gib a beer before settling on the floor, putting his Big Dumb Head directly in front of me and swaying back and forth until I clamber atop him to get a view of:

History in the Making.

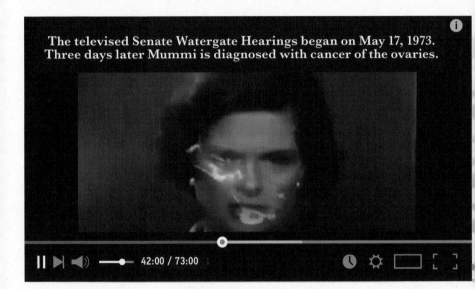

The televised Senate Watergate Hearings began on May 17, 1973.
Three days later Mummi is diagnosed with cancer of the ovaries.

42:00 / 73:00

Inheritance Redux

WHAT I KNOW NOW: though it's obviously been happening for months (actually, years, I will discover much later), I've missed it. And I'm not ready. Perched on the edge of Mummi Lempi's bed, on the edge of hysteria, I call her name, shaking her until

       finally

             finally

quivering with effort, she rises. Propped on an elbow, she blinks slowly, trying to hold her hollowed head upright. Somehow in the twenty-four hours since I last noticed her, she's shed her softness. The hollows and planes of her skull show clearly through the slack skin of her face. Even more terrifying, for the first time in my life, she is

      not

          excited

              to see

                  me.

I can barely speak.

"Mummi Lempi! Are you alright?"

"Yes." She smiles wanly, already turning-turning-turning to lie down again. "I vill get up in a moment."

I flee the dim room and down the hall to my mother.

WHAT I FORGET: Years later when I am diagnosed with fibroids, my mother will remind me of hers, discovered and reported years before.

"I always mail you the results of my annual check-ups," she emails me, "so you know what you're inheriting!"

What kind of bad daughter forgets her inheritance?

WHAT I REMEMBER: Moments of uncharacteristic behavior over the past year (years?). The Saturday Mom said I could have friends over, but Mummi Lempi sent everyone home and drove me back to the farm, hands white–knuckling the steering wheel. The evening a flippant comment sent her running to the car, where she sat in the driveway crying, even after I followed her out to apologize.

Her wan smile the summer of our big cross-country family trip, as she sat in a hotel chair in Boston, and Morfar Gib explained that they were cutting short their trip, but we should continue on, they'd see us at home.

WHAT I DIDN'T UNDERSTAND THEN: The two of us on the living room floor, Mummi Lempi rubbing my back while we wait for our dough sculptures to bake. I lean back into her warm, cinnamon softness and feel her flinch. I turn to find her grimacing.

"I can feel them spreading," she mutters. She shakes her head, speaking more to herself than to me.

"All the things I never said, balled up inside me."

Though I don't understand the words, I recognize the tone. In anyone else, it would be a complaint, but Mummi Lempi never complains, even when she should.

Years later I read in her journal that this was the day she'd pleaded with Doc Rado to test for the cancer she could feel developing inside her.

Minä voin pahoin
I feel sick

WHAT I UNDERSTAND NOW: For months she listened to the quiet rhythms of her body as she worked the garden. Something was shifting in her womb, like the carrot seedlings sprouting through the earth and the top frost melting, like the nissua rising in the oven and calling for touch.

"Go home," Doc Rado told her. He taught her a new English word she looked up in the family dictionary when she got home: *Hypochondria.*

Or was it *Hysteria?*

WHAT'S HARD TO ASK: What were all the things she never said? To the teacher at the English school who kept her after school for talking in class. To the saleswoman who pocketed her money and told the store manager that the little immigrant girl who couldn't speak English hadn't paid. To the voting clerk who ridiculed her accent at the courthouse. To the doctor who ridiculed what she knew about her own body. To Jack, who wouldn't marry her, and Roy, who would but wouldn't stop gambling, and Morfar, a Hothead who did, but later disowned his own daughter and unborn grandchild.

Was cancer the price of being the soft-spoken one among hotheads, the one holding all of us together? As Morfar and Mom battled. As Morfar and Uncle Michael-Väinö battled. As Morfar and Täti Rauha's husbands battled. As Mom and Tant Helen, the hottest of Morfar's hot-tempered sisters, battled. As Mom and I battled. Did she know what was coming?

Was she warning her Black granddaughter not to let silence kill me?

Why I'm Writing In Diaries

> I wonder what [Mother's] job was and how she got along not knowing the language. I remember her saying she was around 18 [when she came to the US] but what happened between then and 21, when she married? Maybe that's why I'm writing in diaries.
>
> —*Mummi Lempi's Diary, 1973*

There are two kinds of people willing to read cancer diaries. Someone who has or had cancer, and someone in love with someone who has or had cancer. Fortunately for the publishing industry and for the author-patient who wants to write a cancer diary, that's a pretty big demographic. Also unfortunately. Because cancer is not a literacy anyone willingly acquires.

Here we go.

January 20, 1972: Got my grades for GED. All in 90s except math which was 75 or so. Better than I expected.

《❖〈

July 31: Gib and I both went to Doc Rado and he prescribed X-rays for me, upper and lower GIs. I told him I've been having more diarrhea, which I've had off and one for two years or so.

《❖〈

August 7: Went to doctor, found out there was nothing wrong except perhaps nerves.

Ahem, point of correction: "Nothing wrong except perhaps nerves?" For some reason (being intimidated by physicians? writing in a second language? being an immigrant farm wife just now getting her GED?) Mummi Lempi is an unreliable narrator in her own damn journal.

It's not the first time. We've been lying, had to lie, from the minute we reached these shores.

Her standard anemia blooms into full-on exhaustion. For two years she kneads the nissua and set it to rise in a warm oven. She trails the barn cats with a box of rags when their bellies distend and they start looking for a place to drop their litters.

She writes as if possessed in her diary. Occasionally, when the pain is too much, she returns to Doc Rado, leaving herself plenty of time to get dinner on the table by five o'clock.

For two years he sends her home with amber-colored bottles of Valium/estrogen/multivitamins, until it's all over her face, something more than hysteria.

«◦»

May 21, 1973 (1 day after the Watergate hearings begin): I had an appointment at 2:30 with Rado. He said I had a growth in my abdomen and scheduled a lower GI, sigmoid and blood tests. Horrors! Castor oil and enemas! The sigmoid test too painful and left me sorer than ever. Couldn't get far from the bathroom all week and didn't feel much like eating.

«◦»

May 26: Went to Rado's and found out that the tumor isn't in my intestine, which was a relief, but I'll have to have a hysterectomy. Pap isn't back or blood test. Had surgery for cancer of the ovaries which had spread in my abdomen. Gib and I went to see Dr. Fletcher, a cancer specialist at the Oregon Medical School. I spent a week at a hospital there for radioactive injection and tests. They put me on chemo which made me nauseous for a week until they cut the dose. Then I felt pretty well except for having less energy and pain if I twisted or turned or bent over. Also depressed but gradually felt better.

«❧‹

"Pretty well . . . except for . . . pain if I twisted or turned or bent over. Also depressed"—a condition that runs in the family, even when we're not dying of cancer. It hurts to read about the pain she didn't voice aloud, to see her blame herself, to imagine her bumping over roads during all the long drives to Portland, three to four hours through the reservation and twisty mountain roads, down to Oregon and along the Columbia River, past waterfalls and locks, normally so beautiful.

«❧‹

June: Had surgery Friday. Lost 11 pounds which was all to the good. Nice to have the family visit and hear what's going on. What do people do without families! Quite a shock to find it was cancer and they didn't get it all. But if all goes well and my blood is in good condition we can go to Portland Medical School for some new chemical treatment or maybe radium. Just have to fight as long as I can. Does no good to wish I had gone to the doctor sooner. It was only a month or so ago that I noticed several new symptoms. Just had a general feeling of tiredness, which I often had before. Cancer is certainly the sneak disease.

≪◈≺

June 15: Spent the afternoon at Rado's waiting for Dr. Fletcher to call from Portland. When he did it was only to say they were out of radioactive stuff. So we're still waiting. No, that was Monday. Friday he didn't even call.

≪◈≺

June 20: I made an angel food cake with thickened cherries. I can do about one thing besides take a bath each day.

≪◈≺

June 24: Tomorrow maybe we'll find out when we leave for Portland. Found out the doctor had called on Friday but Rado didn't call us. Talk about arrogant doctors or maybe absent-minded.

≪◈≺

June 26: Now that we are really going I'm beginning to get nervous. What's to be nervous about? It either works or it doesn't. At least it's a try and they are evidently good at it.

≪◈≺

June 29: They gave me the radioactive phosphorus with a needle in the abdomen. Pretty painful when they hit a nerve, otherwise not bad. Just like an operation, the pain is just as bad. Needed two pain pills. Twenty-eight days since surgery.

«⋙‹

July 4: Lots of pain. Then Holly and Faith surprised us by coming in. It was like a shot in the arm to see them. They stayed till 7:30 when Gib took them to the bus station.

«⋙‹

My mother and I were ending our big train trip Back East and rather than returning directly to Washington, Mom decided to reroute us through Portland, so we could spend the day with Mummi Lempi. I liked the view of the rusty bridges and rivers from the large hospital windows but not the smell, and by the time Morfar Gib made the same journey six years later, I knew that Oregon hospitalization meant eventual death.

If we were salmon, Portland would be our family spawning ground, where my grandparents came of age and met, where they returned to die.

«⋙‹

July 30: Had another blood test and count is low so can't go back on the pills, too much radiation.

Possessed Redux

As she begins to die, Mummi Lempi draws family trees in the back of her diary. She notes milestones for each year. Her lists are big and small, political and personal. In one journal she devotes entire pages to feverish lists of every song she can remember from her youth, interspersed with major historical events. Always busy, now she is possessed. Possessed to archive her world.

It's the same way I write. The same way I teach memoir. The same way I make a film to call her forth from the Underworld, weaving a spell of *Kalevala*, lists, smells, sounds, tastes, talismans. Her diaries are the archive, the spell, the map she leaves me to decipher.

«⋙≺

Movies were still silent with Rudolph Valentino, Douglas Fairbanks, Mary Pickford, Charlie Chaplin, the Barrymores, Gloria Swanson. People were drinking moonshine and several thousand died because it wasn't made right (1926). The movies became talkies and they made lots of musicals. I was 13 years old. The first talkie I saw was Al Jolson in The Singing Fool.

«⋙≺

Her first talkie was Jolson's second film, the follow-up to the loosely autobiographical *The Jazz Singer* about a singer torn between his Jewish identity and his hunger for fame. Both Jolson and his character got their wish, with the actor becoming one of the most famous Jewish Americans of his time, thanks, er, to Blackface.

《❀〉

Little White Lies,
My Buddy,
Moonlight & Roses,
When the Saints,
St. Louis Blues,
12th Street Rag were played when I first went dancing.
Also Melancholy Baby,
Darktown Strutter's Ball,
Lullaby of Broadway,
Lady in Red,
Begin the Beguine,
and usually the last dance, Goodnight Sweetheart.

《❀〉

I only remember Swedish and Finnish folk dances and country music emanating from the long stereo console in the living room. Who was this young woman who shifted from a folksy Swedish hambo with its smooth turns to a fast-traveling two-step accompanied by Black standards like "St. Louis Blues" and "Darktown Strutter's Ball?" Was she Roaring Twenties 'woke?

《❀〉

In 1928 businesses were going broke and in another year the stock market crashed, banks closed and jobs were hard to come by. "Without a Song" and "Stardust" came out that year. I was 17 (1930) and pretty well off because I had a job in a cafeteria and so did Rauha and Väinö.

❮❮❦❯

The cafeteria was Leighton's, where the employees voted her Portland Snow Princess. She didn't mind, because she got to attend lunches and dances but, unlike the Snow Queen, "didn't have to make any speeches." Classic, quiet Mummi. Was she humming these songs as she scribbled and recalled everything from memory? Are the pages saturated with her reluctant voice, like a love letter misted with perfume?

❮❮❦❯

The Depression and Prohibition ended and beer parlors sprang up everywhere. Astaire and Rogers danced and sang in many musicals. "Blue Moon" and "The Continental" were popular songs. We granted independence to the Philippines. Social Security was started in 1936 and the Republicans said it would never last but I notice they are glad to get it now. In 1939 nylon was invented and stockings lasted for years. So they made weaker ones so they could sell more.

❮❮❦❯

There were many good movies taken from good books: *Mutiny on the Bounty*—Clark Gable; *Anna Karenina*—Garbo; *Les Miserables*—Frederic Marsh; *Dead End, The Thin Man* series—William Powell & Jean Harlow; *It Happened One Night*—Gable & Colbert; *Lost Horizon*—Ronald Colman. In 1939 I went to the World's Fair in San Francisco with Roy. Hitler invaded Poland, and England also got into the war but we thought the US wouldn't and we didn't until December 1941 when Japan attacked us.

Roy was her first husband, the Swedish-American gambler she married after it became painfully clear that her true love Jack wasn't going to marry her, even once he could afford to. All those backstreet abortions waiting for the Great Depression to end and Jack to prove that he loved her as much as he said.

By March 1942, three years after going to the World's Fair with Roy, she was already married to her second Swedish-American husband— Morfar Gib—and pregnant with Mom in an unsuccessful attempt to keep him out of the war.

NORSE CULTURE IS SALMON CULTURE

We're the human equivalent of salmon. The farm stinks of the Nordic totem: fat, silver-spotted salmon thrusting upstream, slamming themselves over jagged rocks and leaping pounding waterfalls where Morfar Gib, master fisherman, waits.

He's the only whiteman but not the star, a visitor to the Rez, this nation-within-a-nateion. Yakama and Umatilla fishermen cluster on the scaffolds cantilevered across the falls, long-handle dip nets in hand, squat in small boats, wooden spears at the ready.

CHINOOK (ONCORHYNCHUS TSHAWYTSCHA): The largest, fattiest salmon. Comes in deep-red and white. Can reach up to 135 pounds. Nickname: King Salmon, for obvious reasons.

SOCKEYE (ONCORHYNCHUS NERKA): Second fattiest salmon. requires a lake system for spawing. Nicknames: Red Salmon, Blueback, Silver "Trout".

Natal Homing

Finally, like our people and salmon do, a glassy-eyed Mummi Lempi fights her way upstream, asking for what she wants before death: to go home. Not Finland-home. Not Portland-home. Not Duluth, Minnesota-home. Not Ashtabula, Ohio-home. None of the places the family had settled and fled in the quest to become American. But Lanesville, a tiny hamlet near Rockport, Massachusetts, home for a single childhood year.

The three rooms above her mother's café. The front windows facing Main Street. And further out, the breakwater that protects the fishing boats.

Mom and I decide to accompany Mummi and Morfar for part of the trip, which will be by train (our favorite). The four of us will go to Chicago, then while Mummi and Morfar visit Finnish cousins, Mom and I will branch off to do an American History tour. It's the summer after fifth grade, and I'm obsessed with living museums. I want to visit Colonial Williamsburg,

MORE SALMON

COHO (ONCORHYNCHUS KISUTCH): Found in the coastal waters of Alaska. Large, irregular spots on its back. Nickname: Silver Salmon.

CHUM (ONCORHYNCHUS KETA): The male develops large teeth during spawning, which resemble canine teeth. Nickname: Dog Salmon

PINK (ONCORHYNCHUS GORBUSCHA): The smallest of the Pacific Salmon, up to 12 pounds. The male develops a large hump on its back during spawning. Only runs in odd-numbered years. Nicknames: Humpback Salmon, or if you're on more intimate terms, Humpie.

It's a bittersweet project, the successful return home. A salmon spends her days journeying from the Pacific Ocean to the Columbia river, this spawning and birthing of the next generation accompanied by the exhausted salmon-parents' death. That is, if Morfar and the Native fishermen don't get to them first.

Historic Jamestown, the Freedom Trail where Crispus Attucks was shot. Afterwards, we'll all meet up in Boston. While I read Newbury classic, *Johnny Tremain,* Mummi writes in her diary.

«❧«

May 28, 1974: Getting ready for our trip. Can't make up my mind yet where to go. There are so many places of interest but Lanesville and Detroit and Boston are some.

«❧«

June 4: Went to Rauha's for a cup of tea. She had a letter from Finland and wants to go there this summer. Kind of wish I could, too.

«❧«

June: Holly, Faith, Gib, and I took the train back East. We went to museums in Chicago, then they went to Lincoln's birthplace, Washington, DC, and Richmond while Gib and I went to Detroit to visit Cousin Aileen and Cap.

«❧«

June 17: We flew to Boston, rented a car, and toured Cape Ann where I used to live. Stayed all night in Rockport in an old inn and drove around the island. Found Lanesville and Plum Cove where we used to swim and play when I was 9 and 10. Our restaurant is now an antique shop and there are more houses and trees than before. Rockport is an artists' colony with curio shops everywhere and fishing boats. Lots of lobster fishermen. It stays warm in the evening so people swim in the ocean at 7:00 and 8:00 just like I remember. Ate fish almost every night, haddock and scallops. The seashore was lovely, weather perfect, and we really enjoyed it. Hated to leave but had to meet Holly and Faith in Boston on Friday.

《❦〈

In Lanesville, fifty years after having left, she locates the house-turned-antique shop and recently painted a fresh coat of gray. It is summer, just as she has always remembered. She snaps a photograph of the exterior (which, years later, I will use to navigate my way from my college in Boston to her childhood) and uncharacteristically bold, asks the manager to go upstairs. She's surprised at how small the space is, how small things are in adulthood.

Despite the pain, she moves smoothly, like Morfar in a darkroom. At the point he has developed the image, where he dips the negative into a water solution to halt further sensitivity to light. At the stage where the image's development is arrested, fixed for posterity. She pauses in the doorway, holds her breath. Otherwise, the image over-develops and eventually fades.

My mother: "You didn't know. She was getting weaker. That's why we went on alone. They cut the trip short in Boston and headed back early."

June 30, 1974: Had an appointment with Doc Rado but he didn't show up.

«◦»

Who was this Anti-Doc Rado, who continued to be Morfar's physician after he failed us, time and time again? I know that Mom, empowered American, refused to see him anymore and raged at Morfar for continuing to do so.

Thirty years after the crime, Google has little to offer the amateur sleuth: The name Rado is Polish, Czech, or German. It's Italian. It's Filipino. It's a Swiss watch brand started by brothers. It means "one who made wheels."

It means "alderman."

It means "great and glorious". It does not.

A history of the town next door to ours, also tiny, also agricultural, lists business activity around the time our family moved to the area: "Two new doctors have established offices: Dr. S. O. Tatkin and DR. Elmer Rado (1949)." Three years later, twelve years before Mummi Lempi's death, one Dr. Rado moves "from Division Street to E. 3rd St. and Ash Avenue." Also, "the Dr. Rado Clinic Building remodeled." A whole clinic. Google's satellites reveal East Third and Ash as a sleepy, sunny corner with two houses, a school and a one-story physical therapy clinic painted sky blue. Nothing worth burning down, if the amateur sleuth were so tempted.

July 26: White count 2.0. Rauha broke the news that she and Dennis were engaged. What a surprise! They've only known each other a few months, maybe two.

❮❮◦❯❮

Mom: "That's how we were able to get a house. Täti Rauha knew Mom was dying, which is probably why she rushed to marry That Pompous Old Coot. And then offered to sell us her house in town."

August: went camping, September went to the seaside with the family. Then back to Portland for my checkup, which was good. Rauha and Dennis got married while we were gone. August was a busy month as we helped Holly pack and Rauha too. Kind of depressed with Holly and Faith living in town. Nothing like having young people around to keep your mind off yourself.

October 1974:

<u>November 1974:</u>   «❦‹ - - «❦‹ - - «❦‹ - - «❦‹ - -

«❦‹ - - «❦‹ - - «❦‹ - - «❦‹ - - «❦‹ - - «❦‹

«❦‹ - - «❦‹ - - «❦‹ - - «❦‹ - - «❦‹ - - «❦‹

<u>December 1974:</u> Holly had Christmas dinner and all I had to do was make pies.

This is the last entry.

What I Don't Know

What happens next.

How much longer she lingers with us.

The days, weeks, perhaps months, she lies in a hospital only a few blocks from our new old house in town, becoming smaller and grayer until I stop visiting, this pain so wide and never-ending that none of us can imagine living past it or trying to muster the energy to continue being a family afterwards.

66:00 / 73:00

How To Speak Finnish Redux

But for six years, the six that matter, I study her. I trail my nose through the yellow farmhouse, from Victory garden to kitchen, from Pink Room to perfumed bedroom. I watch her painting and decorating everything, turning rocks and soap into art. I run my fingers over her textiles, stretch like a cat into her warmth, place my tongue on everything.

67:00 / 73:00

And though I can't hear her real-voice, I hear mine:

> Mummi Lempi, tell me about the time you whacked
> your brother on the head with your doll 'cuz he
> wouldn't play with you and then went crying to your
> äiti that he broke it! About the time you weren't
> afraid to talk in school. Can we paint rocks? Can we
> bake lusikkaleivat, even though it's not Christmas?
> Show me how to make the jam from my raspberry
> patch.

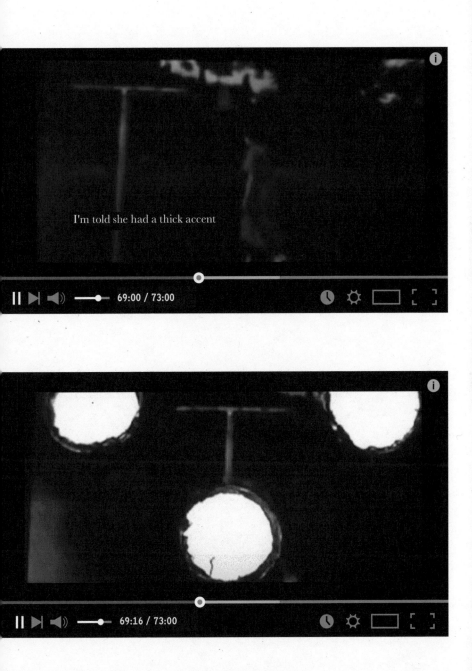

Mummi Lempi, tell me again about the lump in your throat, the one you believe is all the things you never said, collected, now slipping through your bloodstream like poison. I'll listen this time; I promise; I'll understand. Whisper all the things you never said. Tell me about your first husband, Roy the Gambler, and Jack who broke your heart. Tell me about the time your stomach caught fire at the bonfire.

Move inside me; don't ever leave.

Acknowledgments

This slim volume is part of an epic project that involved many years of traveling, finding family, writing, investigating and researching. I was assisted by many people along the way and would like to thank those I remember and apologize to those I've inadvertently omitted.

First and foremost, thank you to my mother for loving books and encouraging me since childhood to be a writer brave enough to tell family secrets. To my husband for understanding that I need to go away to beautiful places to write. To my Finnish cousins who patiently waited a 100 years for our arrival and then welcomed us with open arms.

To my fairy godmother agents, Ayesha Pande and the late Lynn Franklin, both generous and patient. To my writing partner, Elmaz Abinader, and our writing group members Tara Dorabji and Susan Ito, for cheering me on and reading multiple drafts.

To my old Pittsburgh crew, particularly Deesha Philyaw for inviting me to share the John Grisham House while editing the final draft, and T Foley for encouraging me to make the film that inspired this draft and gently pointing out its failures.

To Gabrielle Civil for introducing me to Texas Review Press and reconnecting me with PJ Carlisle, whose brilliant and tireless edits, both written and visual, were an author's dream; to J. Bruce Fuller and PJ for deciding to publish both manuscripts, and to the entire TRP team for taking such care with chapbooks.

Residencies at Write On Door County (Wisconsin) and Cour-Commune (Voulx, France) provided the time and space to envision these projects.

Finally, I am thankful for my colleagues at California College of the Arts, my assistant Anna Alves for handling the stuff I hate so that I can do the stuff I love, and you, dear reader.

What does it mean to lose, and then recreate from fragments of . . . "dreams, film clips, lists, photos, and memories," the beloved voice that has seemingly vanished? *Her Voice* is a poignant, powerful and ultimately triumphant project of inexorable love. A beautiful, breathtaking smorgasbord. . . . A feast for the heart.

—**Susan Kiyo Ito**, author of *I Would Meet You Anywhere: A Memoir*, National Book Critics Circle Award finalist

Faith Adiele has written an astonishing book—[a] coming-of-age memoir—that defies easy classification because it is finally a memoir of the soul. Adiele's witty, painfully candid, and always sharp-eyed account leads the reader to a most profound spiritual and human truth: There is "no easy, static answer" to the question, "What are you?"

—**Richard Rodriguez,** author of *Brown: The Last Discovery of America*

Rooted in childhood, culture, and the diary of her grandmother, *Her Voice*, takes us on a cinematic journey back in time as Adiele searches for home. A hybrid memoir, woven over generations, *Her Voice* is the making of a film and a story of discovery that breathes dreams into reality.

—**Tara Dorabji**, author of *Call Her Freedom*, winner of the Like Us First Novel Prize from Simon & Schuster

Literal fusion: the process of joining two or more things to form a single entity. Innovative, original, Adiele sets off a literary bomb between two worlds, then mines the truth revealed in the explosion.

—**Mat Johnson**, author of *Pym* and *Loving Day*, a New York Times Notable Book, optioned by SHOWTIME

Engrossing, original. Adiele ushers us into the complications of race and identity in the 21st century.

—**Toi Derricotte**, author of *The Black Notebooks*